IT's ALL RIGHT...

Debra P. Raisner • Glenn S. Klausner • David H. Raisner

didit press

Andrews and McMeel
A Universal Press Syndicate Company
Kansas City

illustrations by Frank W. Dormer

layout and typesetting by Steve Brooker at *Just Your Type*

ISBN: 0-8362-2575-9

Library of Congress Catalog Card Number: 96-85620

Lisa Berman and Jason Raisner

*Thank you for your ideas,
encouragement, and creativity*

Special Thanks to

Joel Jacobi, Aimee Kutz, and Tom Valuk

Uncle Harvey & Aunt Elaine, *you* helped us "DO IT"

INTRODUCTION

Who says it's not *all right* to eat dinner foods for breakfast, go on vacation and not bring back gifts for everyone you know, accept gas money, or bring your lunch to work? Who says you can't frame a picture of yourself, take extra samples at the supermarket, or head straight for the sale rack?

Who set these standards, these guidelines, these rules? Why are we all so worried by what everybody else thinks? *It's All Right* reverses the rules and puts us all on the same playing field.

Imagine if the local drugstore sold eyeglasses that gave everyone a new vision and perspective on life—glasses that redefine "embarrassing," normalize life's crazy habits, and show us that the little things we do, but feel guilty about doing...are *all right*.

4

It's All Right gives us that new prescription and provides us with the vision we've all been looking for. It will make you laugh at your reluctance and be comfortable about your desires.

It's All Right assures you that it simply is **all right** to throw your popcorn bucket away after the movies, pass on your mother-in-law's stuffed cabbage, not to have plans for a Saturday night, or dream about lottery winnings. With *It's All Right*, you will feel confident to know that you are not the only one who blushes when forced to ask your host for another roll of toilet paper.

leave the house
without makeup

bring your own
candy to the movies

* * *

raise your hand first

buy
generic products

cry while watching television

mispronounce
someone's name

fake being surprised at
your own surprise party

•••

write your own
wedding vows

turn your phone ringer
off during dinner

read dirty magazines

...

cry out loud

hold in your stomach

be alone

* * *

take seconds

say "I'm tired"

reveal your weight

...

say "I don't understand"

lose

return your
soda cans

accept a compliment

dream

...

take the *last* dinner roll

be laid off

rent

...

use an umbrella

use a night light

practice dancing
in front of the mirror

* * *

wonder if there is a G_d

fall asleep
in a movie theater

be single

***

ask for directions

cry while watching
a movie

eat dinner foods
for breakfast

use the men's room
when the women's line
is too long

have a bad hair day

...

accept gifts

hold hands in public

misunderstand what
someone is saying

...

think "Rush is right"

lose your train
of thought

wear a bathing cap

...

admit you're wrong

apologize

mispell a word

...

wear a girdle

take your clothes off
in front of your doctor

not have plans on a Saturday night

ask for seconds

look up a word
in the dictionary

• • •

cook with Joan

have a woman
pay for dinner

leave less than
15 percent when
the service is poor

...

like your
driver's license picture

hug a male friend

work late

take your parents
to the movies

take a nap

...

walk around your
house naked

IT'S ALL RIGHT TO . . .

be yourself

wear goggles in a racquetball game

hold a grudge

wear white after
Labor Day

* * *

forget the name of the
last book you read

forget the name
of the last movie
you saw

miss an easy
trivia question

• • •

blurt out words that
mean nothing

talk to yourself

let go of someone

...

pick your nose

be confused

mess up on a
job interview

...

have an
embarrassing mother

mispronounce a
menu item

change your own oil

spill your drink

order extra hot fudge
on your sundae

* * *

share your creativity

forget someone's name

be uncomfortable when
reading out loud

...

not know a famous
actress or actor's name

not know the name
of a popular song

not understand what
someone is saying

. . .

change your answering
machine message often

wear clip-ons

mispronounce a word
while reading out loud

...

not know the singer
of a popular song

say I love you

be the first
on the dance floor

sleep naked

get up and leave when
you have had enough

...

speak your mind

listen to Howard

miss a belt loop

* * *

leave your shirt
untucked

help yourself at
someone's house

have a housekeeper

* * *

kiss your parents
in public

take the *first*
dinner roll

have a pimple

● ● ●

color your hair

feel like you are
losing your hair

not match

be last in line

be the first to put your
napkin in your lap

...

not have a date

say your prayers
before bed

swear

...

make love with
the lights on

excuse yourself to
use the bathroom

sing with Rosie O'

•••

feel like you are
too short

feel like you
don't know where
your life is going

eat Lucky Charms
without milk

...

pat yourself on the back

read the dictionary

exit the elevator before every woman has exited

say "I'm leaving"

feel like you are too tall

• • •

talk to strangers

trip on a date

leave food on your plate

* * *

finish everything
on your plate

laugh out loud

express your feelings

• • •

wash your dog
in the shower

be nervous

talk to your pets

...

be shy

feel blue

be lost on the Internet

be uncomfortable
during a lull in
conversation

feel like you
are overweight

* * *

reveal your age

"pass wind"

be the shortest
in a crowd

...

be the tallest in a crowd

write to Ann

have never been
out of the country

...

crack your knuckles

feel important

ask to be reseated

...

sing sit-com themes

introduce yourself to
your waitperson

stick a knife in the
ketchup bottle

* * *

still drink Bud

bite your nails

look in the tissue after
blowing your nose

...

bite ice cream
rather than lick it

be scared when
the plane is going
through turbulence

use coupons

clown around with a
friend in public

kiss your partner for
longer than a peck
in public

• • •

be "fashionably" late

use a bath towel
for more than
one day in a row

sing in the shower

...

own more than one pair
of tennis shoes

only read the headlines
in the newspaper

smell the perfume
in magazines

* * *

give foot massages

just read
the cartoons in
the *New Yorker*
magazine

Stay up Late Night with David

...

not return messages the same day

wear colored contacts

dream about being with
someone famous

...

yell and scream at
the TV during a
sporting event

go to a nude beach

throw your popcorn bucket away after the movie

pick the top off
the crumb cake

wear your underwear
inside-out when you
run out of clean ones

•••

pass on your
mother-in-law's
stuffed cabbage

be sarcastic

use the elevator/escalator
rather than the stairs

•••

watch TV rather than
read a book

see the movie rather
than read the book

make a decision without consulting others

◆ ◆ ◆

watch cartoons on Saturday mornings

cram for a test

let someone switch
into your lane

* * *

cry over a lost love

enter through
the exit door

listen to country music

...

diet with
Oprah and Rosie

press the snooze button
more than once

make a sandwich out of your food

square dance

fall asleep
with the TV on

• • •

ask your boss about
your performance

ask for a raise

disagree

...

tell a bad joke

take a long walk home

worry about
your parents

* * *

admit to telling a lie

board the plane
before they call
your row number

ask for a discount

...

clean for the
cleaning lady

cut your food into
pieces

nominate Oprah
for president

* * *

pay your bills
a little early

wear the same pants
two days in a row

use an iron off the tee

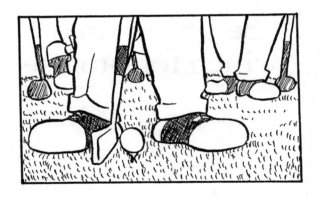

be uncertain of
which fork to use

eat alone in a restaurant

•••

not know the
silverware setup

smile for no reason

feel like you have
big feet

* * *

sweat

have gray hair

buy clothes
at a thrift shop

* * *

go to a wedding alone

give a wedding gift that
is not on the registry

celebrate
Groundhog Day

...

not have an
answering machine

have acrylic nails

not have "call-waiting"

* * *

re-give a gift

oversleep

bring your own
salad dressing

send a belated
birthday card

use comics as
wrapping paper

...

doodle

enter mail-in contests

expect to win

* * *

have a crush
on a movie star

use a map

check your
answering machine
throughout the day

* * *

like a song
on the Top 40

like a song
not on the Top 40

pretend you're talking
on a cellular phone

...

crumble crackers
into your soup

dunk your bread

sleep with
the hall light on

* * *

start a book
and not finish it

walk out of a movie

take a doggie bag

only read the comics

only look at the pictures

• • •

travel to outlet stores

get a second opinion

have student loans

...

chip in for gas

accept gas money

pay someone else's toll

...

accept toll money

sleep with the door
half-open

ask questions

...

drive the speed limit

ask for the price
when the waitperson
announces the specials

ask how much a
doctor's visit will be

• • •

take your parents
out for dinner

take a friend's parents
out for dinner

ask for a taste of more than one ice cream flavor

rename your child
after he/she is born

wear a suit
at a black-tie affair

...

laugh at yourself

pretend

dress comfortably

• • •

be early

never take sick days

be at work on time

• • •

work through lunch

go to church

go to temple

* * *

wear white socks
with dark shoes

sleep with one foot
under the sheets
and one out

forget the name of the person you were *just* introduced to

• • •

wear a seat belt

be nervous
on a first date

wear polyester

...

have a two-handed
backhand

be a lefty

take the hotel soap

wear a seat belt
in the backseat

drink tap water

...

snore

wear a helmet
on a moped

go to a full-service
gas station

...

self-service your gas
even if you own a
luxury car

return your shopping cart

put baking soda
in the refrigerator

...

ask for assistance

let a coach coach in a
Little League game

daydream

* * *

store batteries
in the refrigerator

have dirty running
shoes

wear a reflector vest
while biking

...

bring your parents
to your office

read an encyclopedia

be unable to pronounce the wines on the wine list

read a thesaurus

go back to night school

...

not laugh at a joke

be confused at the
beginning of a book

call your mother
when you feel blue

...

send a meal back
in a restaurant

have an unbalanced
checkbook

share a can of soda

...

admit you're sleeping
when someone
wakes you

jump in a puddle

let your child play
under the clothes racks

...

not enjoy your vacation

leave a
vacation spot early

set your
clock/watch ahead

...

reposition the golf ball
while playing
miniature golf

play jacks

wear sneakers with a suit to work

dance on a table

live with your parents

...

use the Yellow Pages

buy a mattress
over the phone

take a lot of pictures
on vacation

· · ·

give your dog
people food

keep a journal

wear two
different-colored socks

• • •

introduce yourself first

buy a used car

sleep past noon

•••

put postcards in your
photo album

use dandruff shampoo

brush your teeth
in the shower

* * *

shave in the shower

have a stuffed animal

use your refrigerator as a photo album

keep the picture in the
frame you just bought

wear cheap sunglasses

. . .

have a stage name

eat burnt toast

talk to your plants

* * *

revisit a vacation spot

skip

go to the movies alone

• • •

buy yourself flowers

be a Republican and
vote Democrat

buy a used
wedding gown

...

wear a ski hat

believe your horoscope

wear corduroy

* * *

get lost while driving

IT'S ALL RIGHT TO . . .

work two jobs

cheer for the away team

ask questions

fall in love

...

be in a parade

tape soap operas

be kosher

...

eat cookies in bed

picnic with your
family at the beach

wear pajamas

• • •

have never flown
on a plane

put the milk
back in the refrigerator
with only a drop left

play in the rain

• • •

say you baked it, when
it's really Sara Lee

sing along with the
radio in the car

pray for a miracle

* * *

dream about lottery winnings

toss coins into a
wishing well

split the bill

alphabetize your CDs

put hot fudge, M&M's,
and whipped cream
on frozen yogurt

• • •

wear bifocals

save your gum

screen your phone calls

...

channel surf repeatedly,
even though you know
nothing's changed

jump in a pile of leaves

vacation without
your kids

...

wear bikini bottoms
when you run out of
underwear

get your palm read

ask for a second date,
ten minutes into
the first one

...

flirt

talk about the weather

slip on ice

...

blow bubbles

use someone else's
toothbrush

take the penny when the item costs 99¢

IT'S ALL RIGHT TO . . .

be a bad dancer

kiss on the first date

. . .

go to therapy

have a messy car

have dark roots

...

ask the waiter for the
salad dressings...again

smell your T-shirt

go to the circus
without kids

...

go *back* to the salad bar

drink white wine
with red meat

forget who won
the last World Series

...

pull an "all nighter"

not do the dishes
right after dinner

lock your keys in the car

...

be pale at the beach

eat cookie dough

be broke

skip a day when dieting

hold hands with your
mother

• • •

fall asleep in church

run out of gas

be a bad cook

...

vacation without
your spouse

IT'S ALL RIGHT TO . . .

head straight for the
sale rack

go out with the "girls"

* * *

go out with the "guys"

bring your lunch

have your eye makeup
smudge

• • •

go to the racetrack
for the food

be politically incorrect

go on vacation and not
bring gifts back for
everyone you know

* * *

think the Taj Mahal
is only a casino in
Atlantic City

tell someone they ran
out of toilet paper

be uninterested in what's going on in professional sports

like your haircut

complain about smokers

. . .

be first to call after a
first date

drink champagne
from a plastic cup

bring your pillow
on a car ride

•••

wear costume jewelry

pick out your clothes
the night before

enjoy A.M. radio

...

have a crush
on your doctor

like the dentist's
toothpaste

not refill the
ice cube tray

...

brush your teeth with
warm water

drive when you
could have walked

wear a bike helmet

take a family portrait

use sunblock
in a tanning booth

. . .

buy jewelry from QVC

stop at a
yellow traffic light

be religious

...

wear nonprescription
eyeglasses

wear earmuffs

order half regular/
half diet

•••

step in "number 2"

share an ice-cream cone
with your dog

sneeze during a
group meeting

* * *

wear a baseball cap
when you
haven't showered

IT'S ALL RIGHT TO . . .

call in sick
even when you're not

work on the weekends

...

pluck your gray hairs

go to bed early

wear inline skating pads

drink cheap wine

pick a nickname
for yourself

* * *

use spell-check

iron your
dry-cleaning clothes

have twenty
"best friends"

• • •

lather, rinse, and
not repeat

admit you like money

sing louder than the
song you are listening to

...

put the carrot tongs
in the cucumber bowl
at the salad bar

take a bath

take a job for lesser pay

...

make a wish

think that
J. Edgar Hoover
invented the vacuum

wear Wranglers

* * *

judge a book
by its cover

ask for just a little ice
in your soft drink

kiss with
your eyes open

take your shoes
off at work

work third shift

...

be the loudest parent
in the stands

eat a plain bagel

make your bed
in the morning

• • •

have nasal hair

read romance novels

watch soap operas

* * *

read in the bathroom
at work

visit the house
you grew up in

save your change

...

be a house-husband

go on a blind date

exercise in the morning

...

beat your boss in golf

vacation in your backyard

take extra samples
at the supermarket

get a third opinion

trick-or-treat
at age thirty

• • •

extend your vacation

ask your host
what they prepared
for dinner

go barefoot

...

call the psychic hotline

be impatient

ask the pharmacist
where the condoms are

• • •

make believe you
understood the opera

admit to using
the Thigh Master

slurp your soup

...

smell your food
before you taste it

be a vegetarian

use a fork rather than
chopsticks

• • •

read poetry

ask the flight attendant
for more peanuts

clean up after your dog in public

be romantic

kiss your sister

. . .

let your mother think
she's a photographer

unbutton your top button

eat sushi
with your fingers

* * *

tell your grandparents
they are your friends

IT'S ALL RIGHT TO . . .

eat veggies for a snack

wear a bow tie

...

read *Reader's Digest*

get a makeover
in the mall

say no thank you

• • •

wear a bib

not have a beeper

bring your own coffee
cup to the coffee shop

...

carry a comb in your
back pocket

read yesterday's paper

take the bigger piece

wait for the walk signal

tell people
it's your birthday

...

still tie your sneakers
with bunny ears

think you
look good

practice your autograph

IT'S ALL RIGHT TO . . .

temp

frame a picture
of yourself

IT'S ALL RIGHT TO . . .

disagree
with the authors

We would like to hear from you! If you disagree with any of the *It's All Rights* or have any comments, feel free to let us know. Write to us at: P.O. Box 923, Brookline, MA 02146, or through our web site at: http://www.diditpress.com.

374